RICKY MARTIN

By Maggie Marron

RICKY MARTIN

By Maggie Marron

BARNES
&NOBLE
BOOKS

Dedication

For Maria Tahim, who lives the crazy life

A FRIEDMAN GROUP BOOK

Copyright ©1999 by Michael Friedman Publishing Group, Inc.

Library of Congress Cataloging-in-Publication Data available upon request.

ISBN 1-56799-916-6

Editor: Emily Zelner
Designer: Jennifer O'Connor
Photography Editor: Valerie E. Kennedy
Production Manager: Richela Fabian

Color separations by Radstock
Printed in England by Butler & Tanner

10 9 8 7 6 5 4 3 2 1

Michael Friedman Publishing Group
15 West 26 Street
New York, NY 10010

Contents

Introduction

After Ricky Martin delivered his performance of "La Copa de la Vida" at the 1998 Grammy Awards in February 1999, host Rosie O'Donnell quipped, "I never heard of him before tonight, but I'm enjoying him s-o-o much." Ricky caught everyone off guard that night when he gyrated his "cutie patootie" around the stage of the Shrine Auditorium in Los Angeles in tight leather pants, exuding his raw, unbridled sexuality. Who could resist such energy, such passion? Certainly not the Grammy audience, which responded with thunderous applause and a standing ovation for the "Latin King."

But, of course, we had heard of him before. Grown-up Menudo fans may remember him as tiny Ricky, "the little cute one." Soap opera fans might remember lusting after Miguel Morez, the singing bartender on *General Hospital*. Theater devotees might remember Ricky as Marius, the young idealist, from his Broadway stint in *Les Misérables*. And who's that guy who sings and dances through the TV commercials for Puerto Rico tourism? Yes, that's right—it's Ricky.

Mainstream American audiences are just getting to know this Latin icon, who has already taken the rest of the world by storm, playing sold-out concerts in his native Puerto Rico, as well as exotic locales like Bejing, Singapore, and Australia. His first four albums have sold more than 15 million copies combined worldwide. His Grammy performance boosted sales of his fourth album, *Vuelve,* 500 percent–talk about a career-affirming couple of minutes!

Ricky strikes a pose.

Mucho Charisma

But Ricky is more than just a sexy body, a powerful voice, an electrifying dancer, and a devastatingly handsome guy. He's a real person, who is as intelligent as he is good-looking, as confident as he is talented. His fan base is as diverse as can be: women and men of all ages, backgrounds, and ethnicities. "Ricky's absolutely electrifying," Sony president Tommy Mottola told *People* magazine. "He's got this special charisma that only comes along once in a while."

Confident and self-assured without being arrogant, cocky, or pretentious, Ricky's about as down-to-earth as you can get. "My favorite foods are all fattening," he confided to *Seventeen*. "And I'm really bad at sports. I don't know how to play anything." He doesn't stand on ceremony and he doesn't expect the star treatment. "Everyone is telling me I have to do this and do that," he told *People*. "I'm like, 'Argh! Give me the cheap shampoo and the hotel soap.'"

Ricky's really excited about the opportunity to burst onto the American music scene—although his first love will always be Puerto Rico. "It's all about communication," he says. "I've done recordings in French, in Portuguese—why not English? I'll never stop singing in Spanish. I'm very proud of where I come from. But let's communicate, right?"

Now that he's finally made the crossover, just who is this mild-mannered Latin king?

Ricky Martin smiles, showing off his first English language CD at Tower Records in New York City.

More than 6,000 fans turned out for Ricky's signing on May 11, 1999 at Tower Records in New York City. Here, female fans hold up signs to get Ricky's attention.

CHAPTER ONE

El Niño

Enrique Martin Morales was born in San Juan, Puerto Rico, on Christmas Eve 1971. His early years were marred by the unhappy marriage of his parents, Enrique Martin, a psychologist, and Nereida Morales, a legal secretary. In 1973 the couple divorced and agreed to share custody of the baby Enrique.

The joint custody arrangement proved to be much more complicated than it seemed at the time. Ricky's parents continued their constant sparring and were downright selfish about how much time each of them wanted to spend with their son. Both were so taken by the delightful baby that neither parent wanted to share little Enrique.

The struggle became increasingly hard on Enrique, but he got by, leading as normal a life as he could under the circumstances. While he bounced back and forth between his parents, he escaped from his real life into the magical world of television. That's when Ricky realized what he wanted to do. At age eight, he got into TV commercials, and for the next few years, he found an escape from his bickering, proprietary parents. When Ricky was twelve, he auditioned for the group Menudo and was accepted. He knew this was the ticket to all of his dreams coming true.

Ricky was initiated into Menudo in 1983, and rode high with the group through their most successful years. Despite the group's rigorous rehearsal and

A young Ricky Martin sings his heart out with Menudo.

A very young Ricky poses with a lucky Menudo fan during his early years with Menudo.

touring schedule and Ricky's intense love both for his parents and Puerto Rico, he was eager to join the band. "I was so enthusiastic about being part of the group that even my parents were surprised about how easily I could distance myself from them. It seemed unreal to them that a child who was so mild-mannered, and loved being home so much, could leave without any regrets."

But he had to break free from his family. The battle for his attention had gotten so intense by the time Ricky hit his teens, he was almost glad to be on the road for three-fourths of the year and working sixteen-hour days when he was home. At one point, his father demanded that Ricky chose between his parents. That was the straw that broke the camel's back. "How do you ask a child to do that?" he wonders even to this day. This created a giant rift between Ricky and his father, and began a silence that lasted more than ten years. At thirteen, Ricky chose to live full time with his mother and her children from her first marriage, and to change his name to Ricky Martin. He decided to have nothing further to do with his father.

While Ricky was with Menudo, the band went international and images of the boys hung on posters in the bedrooms of girls around the world. In 1983, the group triumphantly made the *Guinness Book of World Records* for playing to the largest audience anywhere.

❀ Fan Facts ❀

Name:	**Enrique Martin Morales (changed to Ricky Martin)**
Birthdate:	**December 24, 1971**
Sign:	**Capricorn**
Height:	**6′1″**
Eye color:	**Brown**
Hair color:	**Light brown**
Parents:	**Nereida Morales and Enrique Martin Negroni**
Siblings (step):	**Angel, Vanessa, Fernando, Eric, Daniel**
Favorite actor:	**Robert De Niro**
Favorite movie:	***The Godfather***
Favorite designer:	**Giorgio Armani**
Favorite song:	**"Fragile" by Sting**

Ricky, looking sexy as ever at a signing at Tower Records in Los Angeles.

Ricky in one of his final Menudo performances.

In 1984, Menudo released "Hold Me," their biggest U.S. single. Girls everywhere feasted their eyes on the sexy young teens in the video as they pranced through the streets of Los Angeles dressed in stone-washed jeans and bandannas, led by a lip-licking Ricky, who looked all of four feet tall and seven years old but, even then, was irresistible.

In many ways, Menudo wasn't all it was cracked up to be. True, the boys had international fame and more money than they would ever know what to do with, but the price was high. "From twelve to seventeen, the most important years of anyone's life, I had to ask permission to talk and move and to go places," Ricky recently told *Vanity Fair*. "I learned the real meaning of the word 'discipline.'" But that discipline has served him well. Ricky confessed to *People* in 1995 that "Menudo was the best school. All the rehearsals and the discipline—it was like the military."

Good experience or not, any ex-member would agree that the politics of the group—which were really founder Edgardo Diaz's politics—were oppressive. Diaz was the only one who had any voice. "Our creativity was stifled," Ricky told *People*. "We were told [the songs we wrote] were no good. We began to question the need for rehearsing the same routines over and over." Ultimately, though, because Ricky knows the time he spent in the group has

Menudo:
BEHIND THE SCENES

Menudo was the brainchild of Edgardo Diaz, a musician who created the group in 1977. His idea was to create a following for a group of teenage boys, but to not let anyone stay in the band after they reached the age of seventeen. That way the group would remain forever young, appealing to generations of teenyboppers who couldn't get enough of the boys and their melodies.

By the time Ricky joined the group in 1983, Menudo had already penetrated the English-speaking market and was doing TV specials and a film—but it wasn't until Ricky joined the group that Menudo really took off. That year, Menudo really packed the house—in addition to setting a world record for the largest audience ever: one show in the Azteca Stadium attracted 105,000 fans!

In 1984, Menudo was appointed the International Youth Ambassador for UNICEF, and the boys were in the public eye as role models for staying in school and avoiding drugs. In 1987, Ricky's last year, Menudo's tenth-anniversary tour sold out throughout the United States and Latin America.

Out of all the members of the group, only Ricky and Menudo-mate Robi Rosa (co-writer of "Livin' La Vida Loca," among other top Ricky hits) have managed to survive in the music world.

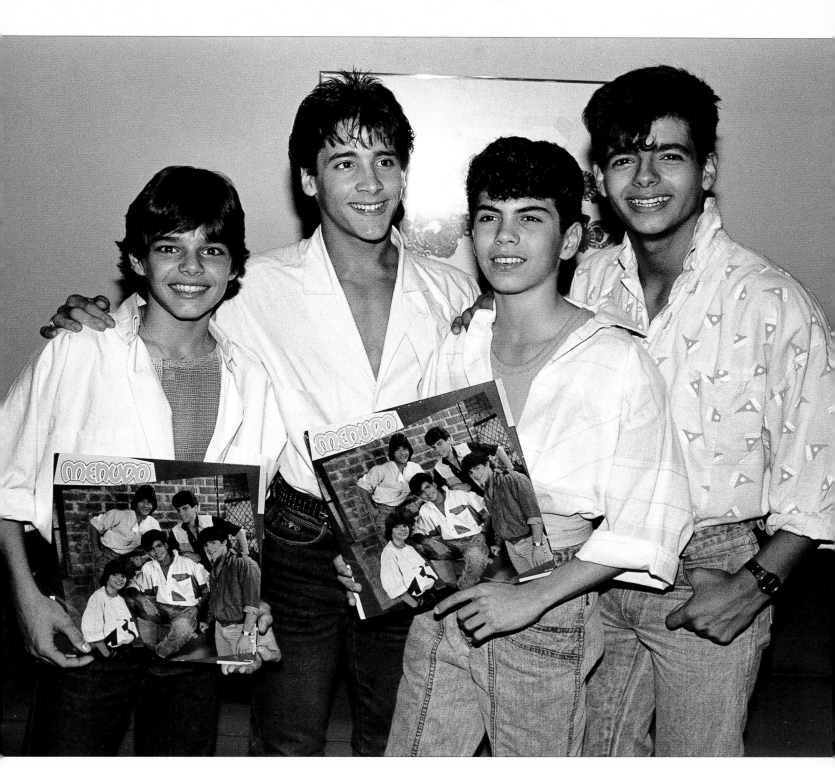

Ricky and the guys show off their American crossover hit record. You can see why they called him "tiny" Ricky!

helped him become the strong performer he is today, he told *Entertainment Weekly*, "For me, it's been easy to forgive."

Besides invaluable training and a sense of professional discipline, Menudo gave Ricky his future producer and collaborator, Robi Rosa, who wholeheartedly agrees with Ricky's philosophy of Menudo. "Two things can happen when you join a group like Menudo," Rosa told *Time* magazine. "You can get all messed up, or you can pay attention and learn from it. We learned a lot. For Ricky and me, the studio is like home now."

On top of the demanding schedule and constant touring that prevented Ricky from enjoying a normal adolescence, it was difficult for him to have normal teenage relationships with girls because he was an international star. He didn't really know any "girls"—at least not the kind you would meet in your chemistry class. Instead, he was always surrounded by grown women. "When I was fourteen, I started to get the chills around older women," he told *People*, "but they would always say, 'Ohh, cute little Ricky!'" Eventually, he and his fellow Menudo mates realized that as superstars, they didn't have to be afraid of girls. "We had many girls," he told *People*. "We'd swap girls." But he grew out of that. (At this writing, Ricky is linked romantically with Spain-based TV presenter Rebecca de Alba.)

Ricky hams it up with Menudo-mates, from left: Sergio Gonzalez, Charlie Rivera, Ricky, Ricky's future producer Robi Rosa, and Ray Acedvedo.

A year later, the Menudo members have changed—the older ones have been forced out to find new careers and only Sergio, Ricky, and Ray remain. Soon Ricky will join the ranks of the ex-Menudos.

Menudo poses with Alyssa Milano, one of the hottest television stars of the late 80s, known for her role as Tony Danza's daughter in Who's the Boss? That's Ricky on the far left.

Coming of Age

The halcyon days of Menudo eventually came to a close. Diaz's age restriction on Menudo members eventually caught up with Ricky, and in 1988, at age seventeen, Ricky found himself out of a job and out of the spotlight. "I gave Menudo all I had," he confessed, "and when I felt it was the moment to part with them, I left completely convinced that I was ready for another stage of both my career and life."

Ricky finished high school in Puerto Rico and then moved to New York to find himself and figure out his next move. "I wanted to get to know myself, because the first five years of my career had been a nonstop barrage of euphoria and adrenaline and a lot of mixed feelings," Ricky told the *Los Angeles Times* in 1998. He didn't do much of anything in New York except loaf around and spend time alone for nearly a year. He had no need to work—Menudo had made him a millionaire—but Ricky is a deep and complicated person and he needed the time to make up for his missed adolescence. "I did a lot of growing up [in New York]," he admitted to *People* in 1995. "In Menudo they told you what silverware to use. Suddenly I was paying my own bills."

It was Ricky's mother who finally helped him get the ball rolling again. "There was only one person who kept telling me, 'You gotta go back on stage.' It was my mother, always there, bugging me the way only she can. And I would tell her, 'Mom, I'm never going back on stage.' It took me only a year to go back," he told the *Los Angeles Times*.

Ricky's childhood was tumultuous, but Ricky emerged from that chaos a wiser, more reflective man. "That young child is still alive," he confesses, "and he has transformed himself into the judge of the man that I have become."

Did you know...
Ricky loves classical music most of all, but also listens to classic rock, salsa, and New Age. Although he counts his song "Fuego de Noche, Nieve de Dia" as one of his favorites, he loves Sting and his song "Fragile" as well as anything by Journey—especially "Faithfully."

Ricky back in concert after leaving the cast of Les Misérables.

CHAPTER TWO

Matinee Idol

Did you know...

Ricky loves to wear the designs of Giorgio Armani, but you'll also see him sporting clothes by Dolce & Gabbana, Helmut Lang, Yohji Yamamoto, and Paul Smith.

Ricky with his dog wrapped around his shoulders. Lucky Dog!

Ricky strums his guitar, composing new material in his bedroom in his Los Angeles home.

Ricky finally got himself focused and motivated, and instead of returning to Puerto Rico, he took off for Mexico City in 1988. He joined another music group called Munecos de Papel, but he didn't stay with them for long. Ricky's childhood dream of being a TV star led him to try to find work as an actor.

Ricky started doing some stage work, but quickly landed a role on a Spanish soap opera, or novella, called *Alcanzar una Estrella* (Reach for a Star), in which he briefly starred. The series spawned a film, and Ricky reprised his role for the big screen. His performance was so well received it earned him a

Heraldo, the Mexican equivalent of an Academy Award. Ricky might have continued acting indefinitely if not for his other love. In 1990, the same year he won his Heraldo, Ricky signed with Sony. He recorded his first album, *Ricky Martin*, in Spanish, and began a concert tour of South America.

Ricky's music was his first priority in the early 1990s, though he continued to take acting jobs when he could. By the time he released his second album, *Mi Amarás*, in 1993, Ricky had the attention of the Latin American community. He was an established recording artist, much-sought-after live performer, TV star, and award-winning actor. He needed to make his next jump. So he packed up his stuff and moved to Los Angeles to pursue acting opportunities there.

In 1994, he crossed paths with Wendy Riche, the executive producer of the long-running soap opera *General Hospital*. Riche had seen Ricky perform and was really drawn into the Ricky mystique when she met him at a party in Los Angeles. She was so impressed by Ricky that she created a role on *General Hospital* for him. "He just lives to perform," she told *Time* magazine.

The role, however, was not a test of his already proven acting abilities. He portrayed Miguel Morez, a singing bartender from Puerto Rico. "For us, Miguel is the essence of who Ricky is," she explained. "He's a very noble, very

Ricky in his yard at his Los Angeles house, springtime 1994.

Ricky poses on his garden fence at his Los Angeles home.

loving character." The role would give Ricky a chance to further develop his abilities as an actor, while giving him a forum to show the U.S. and Canadian public what a talented actor—and singer—he was.

The public devoured him. Riche sensed immediately how popular Ricky would be on the show. "The mail response on him is very positive," she told *People* in May 1995. "Ricky will be very big." That prediction proved dead-on.

Ricky, in his unpretentious, welcoming way, made many friends during his two-year tenure on *General Hospital*, but he was especially close to Lily Melgar, who played his onscreen love interest. "People just love and adore Ricky," Melgar told *People* magazine. "He has a regal presence with the spirit of a child."

But *General Hospital* was not the end of the road for Ricky. He had a whole career yet to play out, and by 1996, he was ready to move on. Ricky has confided that he appreciated that his character wasn't killed off in the show. That way, he would be able to return if he wanted to. Will he want to...? Who knows, this man is full of surprises....

It's very important to Ricky not to get pigeon-holed in a certain role, which is probably why he moves around a lot and is constantly evolving as a performer. But he doesn't really mind being associated with his previous work. "When I left [Menudo], I took a whole year off just to spend time with myself," he confessed in an interview with *Latin Music* online. "When I came back into the 'spotlight' I had a completely different image. In Latin America, they don't remember me as being with Menudo. I was a little kid in Menudo, I had long hair, and it was a different point of view; sometimes I have to remind people where I come from. I don't mind when they ask me about the soap, I think the soap fed the music career and the music fed the acting, like a circular process."

Breaking the Boundaries

As Ricky toiled away in his role as Miguel Morez, he was also hard at work on his third album, *A Medio Vivir*. *A Medio* contains more than one Ricky trademark song: "…well, it has 'Revolucion,' it has 'Maria,' which has more of a Spanish feel to it, a little flamenco, a little cumbia…it has salsa. It was very important for me to do this kind of music because it helps me break boundaries. That's what I want, that's what I need to do. I feel the need to do it because, I'm very lucky, I'm in a career that makes it very easy for me to go to different countries because it's about music. I have to, I want to, keep doing these kinds of rhythms. Hey, I'm Latin. I get the swing of it.

A seductive publicity photo for General Hospital.

A Medio was also a very personal album, one that he was involved in more than the others that came before, or anything he ever did with Menudo. "Everything that you listen to in this album, that's my life. I sat with different composers and told them what I wanted to express; what I was going through at that moment of my life and how I wanted to approach the audience with that album," he reported to *Latin Music* online.

Even though Ricky didn't write any of the songs on *A Medio*, he does like to write a lot of his own material and plans to do a lot of songwriting in the future. "It's beautiful to write, to sing your own music. You know what you're talking about, you know what you're saying. The feeling I get when I'm on stage...I will never change that for anything. It gives you strength, it gives you some kind of power, it gives you control. What do I want to be doing in thirty years? I want to do this. I want to do music."

Ricky was lucky in that he reconnected with Robi Rosa, one of his Menudo-mates, when he made *A Medio Vivir*. Ricky is quite fond of his former bandmate: "I think he's a genius," he told *Latin Music* online. "From the age of twelve, he was always in front of the piano...I remember him. He just recorded his second album. I heard it and it's poetry...it's deep poetry. Musically he has great taste. I mean, you can ask him: 'Robi, let's do

Ricky and co-star (and onscreen love interest) Lily Melgar strike a seductive pose at the 1994 Daytime Emmy Awards.

Ricky as Miguel Morez, the singing bartender, on General Hospital.

something dark, let's do something like 'Maria,' [and] boom.'...He deserves a lot more credit, but you see at the same time he doesn't do music for credit, he does it for himself."

For Ricky, one of the most significant events in 1996 was when he finally ended his estrangement from his father. Now a grown man of twenty-four, Ricky decided there was no reason for him to hold a grudge for a comment that was made in anger and desperation more than ten years before. Ricky admitted he "hated the estrangement, and I just couldn't live with it anymore."

The reconciliation changed Ricky; he says it has made him a better person. "While I was away from my father, I became a cynic. I was cold, sarcastic; I didn't like children. I was a different person. Now, I'm dying to be a father. I actually have more of a desire to be a dad than a husband."

Ricky's next stop: Broadway. He accepted the role of Marius in *Les Misérables*, which began a few months after his last episode of *General Hospital*. In between jobs, Ricky took some much-needed time to regroup. "I need time by myself. I need to spend some time alone; I need to write. I need to find those feelings and just be," he told *Latin Music* online. "I'm always surrounded

Did you know...
Ricky's favorite movie is *The Godfather*, but he loves movies from all over the world, including *Law of Desire*, from Spain, *Il Postino*, from Italy, and the Cuban film *Fresa y Chocolate*.

❧ Les Misérables ❧

When Ricky joined the cast of *Les Misérables* in 1996, he had big shoes to fill. Based on the perennially best-selling novel which was first published in 1865, the musical hit Broadway in 1987. It swept the Tony Awards—winning eight—and even now, is still one of the hottest tickets in town. Although Ricky did not hold the main lead, his role was pivotal to the unfolding of the plot.

Les Misérables tells the story of Jean Valjean, an ex-convict turned factory worker, turned fugitive, and his inner battles between good and evil in a society plagued by the same conflicts. Valjean decides to turn over a new leaf after a bishop, from whom he has stolen silver, lies to save Valjean.

Although he has skipped parole and changed his name, Valjean has taken the straight road, and the story finds him a few years later as a factory owner and town mayor. Valjean inherits his "daughter" Cosette when he promises one of the women who was fired from his factory that he will take care of her daughter when she dies. Still being pursued by Inspector Javert, Valjean is discovered again and must leave without Cosette; years later he comes back to retrieve her.

Valjean and Cosette move to Paris, where they meet Marius (Ricky), a student and a revolutionary. Marius and Cosette fall

The lovers Marius (Ricky) and Cosette dream of a future without political strife in Les Misérables.

Ricky as the student-idealist Marius in Les Misérables.

in love, but when Valjean's past catches up with them, the lovers are separated as Cosette must leave with her father.

Marius gets involved in the Revolution and Valjean knows he is in trouble, so he returns to Paris at his own risk to save him. Valjean rescues an unconscious Marius from the battlefield, but Marius does not know that the person who saved him was the fugitive father of his own beloved. When Valjean is found out yet again, he is saved because of a ring he bears that actually belongs to Marius. Ultimately, the young lovers are married, and Marius discovers that it was Valjean who had rescued him. Valjean dies and joins the spirits of all those sacrificed for the Revolution.

by people. I mean, it's great because they're friends; they're the people that I work with and people that I enjoy spending time with. But I need more time to be alone, just to put my thoughts in order. Just to realize what I'm doing and what I want to do."

When he got back into it, he did it with passion, lending the role of Marius the kind of fire that only Ricky Martin can provide. But the most exciting and challenging times were still ahead of him.

CHAPTER THREE

Singing Sensation

Ricky is the voice of Hercules in the Latin/Spanish version of the Disney animated film. Here he records the soundtrack.

After spending a year pounding the boards in *Les Misérables*, Ricky began work on his most successful album yet, *Vuelve*. The record was finally released in the summer of 1998—and it drove Ricky Martin fans around the world absolutely wild. *Vuelve* went platinum almost instantly. But Ricky fever hadn't really caught on in the United States yet, even though he had a strong following of Spanish Americans. And let's not forget, Ricky had a bevy of devoted fans who had been introduced to him through *General Hospital*; when these new fans realized that they could buy his music, let's just say that it didn't hurt record sales.

Martin's special brand of music originates in his mix of tried-and-true Latin rhythms with current musical trends, plus that last touch of pure Ricky magic. Ricky told *Seventeen* that his "music is fusion. I was raised in Puerto Rico, so I've been influenced by many cultures." *Vuelve* really reflects this mix. Barry Walters of *Rolling Stone* reports that Ricky's "favorite [kinds of] music are classical and classic rock," and confirms that "*Vuelve* mixes the two in a rich stew of pounding percussion, deeply emotional melodicism and ethereal, symphonic sonics." He adds, "You don't need to know a word of his tongue to appreciate the poetry of his performance."

The year 1998 provided Ricky with lots of opportunities to stand out. His song "La Copa de la Vida" (The Cup of Life) was chosen as the theme song for the World Cup competition closing ceremonies on July 12, 1998. Ricky was selected because he exemplified the ideals the organizers wanted to capture in music. Soon the song was everywhere, stealing the thunder from "Maria," his most popular song at the time. "Maria" is obviously a song Ricky loves. "I am going to be singing [it] for the rest of my life," he told *Billboard*. "It gave me direction and logic."

Ricky performed "La Copa de la Vida" for a live audience of 85,000—not to mention the millions more around the world who watched the performance from their living rooms. "Forget about the people in the stadium," Martin told *Seventeen* magazine with a touch of wonder at his own success. "A billion people were sitting at home watching it. I wasn't thinking about that when I stepped on stage. But I wanted to do it so badly, and it turned out very beautiful."

Ironically, while Ricky was performing at the World Cup, several of his former Menudo-mates were on a reunion tour as Reencuentero. Although Ricky appreciated the Menudo experience when it happened, Menudo is strictly a thing of the past

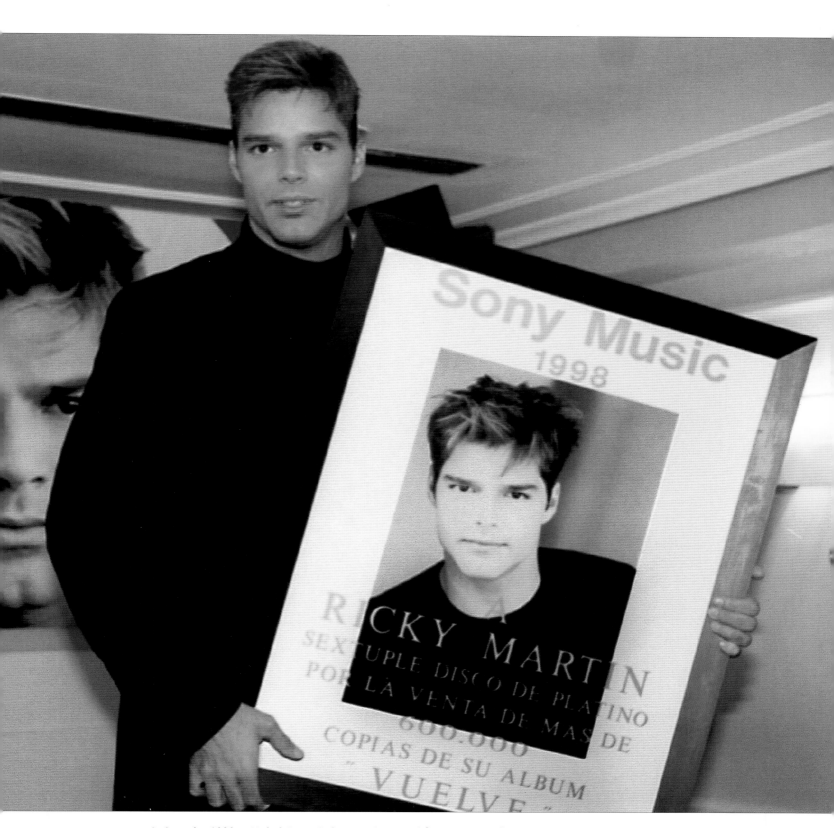

In September 1998 in Madrid, Spain, Ricky received an award from Sony Music for selling 600,000 copies of Vuelve.

Ricky balances the two awards he won at the Billboard *Latin Music Awards in Miami, Florida, in April 1999.*

for him and not something he really ever wants to revisit. "It's something I would never do. But let's be clear about it. I am Latin American and I know how important that group was for a whole generation of people. If everybody is having a good time, if the guys on stage are enjoying it and the people who go see them have fun remembering the old times, I have no problem whatsoever with it." He added: "You know, at this point in the game, I want the stage all for myself. I'm really selfish that way."

Ricky's World Cup anthem was making an even bigger impact on the world than the Latin King could have imagined. It all started with the 100th anniversary of the U.S. invasion of Puerto Rico (which occurred on July 25, 1998). About that time, the governor of Puerto Rico, Pedro Rossells, saw Ricky perform "La Copa de la Vida" on TV, and the governor was so impressed that he chose "La Copa de la Vida" as the theme song for Puerto Rico's quest to become the fifty-first state. Songwriters Desmond Child and Robi Rosa

Did you know...
Ricky is such a good guy that some of his biggest fans are not his audience members but the people who actually work with him: "Ricky is somebody who has taken the required steps into true artistry by tapping into his innermost essence, both musically and philosophically. He is a perfectionist, but at the same time a very trusting man, which is wonderful for a producer. There is no better relationship you can have with an artist," says K.C. Porter, co-producer with Robi Rosa of *Vuelve.*

adamantly insist, however, that the song was written for the World Cup, with the World Cup and only the World Cup in mind and "not to advance the cause of the New Progressive Party (NPP)." In September 1998, Desmond Child told *Billboard* magazine that "the song is strictly about world unity and the World Cup. We weren't rooting for anybody. It was meant to be about games and sportsmanship."

The NPP admits they had not requested permission from Ricky to use the song but, according to Angelo Medina, Martin's manager and a known statehood advocate, Ricky isn't bothered by it. Medina says Ricky is pleased to use his image to enhance Puerto Rico's image, which is what Ricky is all about.

On Sept 3, 1998, Ricky became the Puerto Rico Board of Tourism's official spokesperson in a "new campaign designed to focus more on the warmth of the people of Puerto Rico." What better spokesperson could there be than the dashing, sexy, sweet-spoken Martin? The commercials hit the air on September 14, 1998, priming a Ricky-ready audience for his storming of the United States.

In October, before Ricky set out on his tour to promote *Vuelve*, he helped launch a Puerto Rican theme restaurant in South Beach, Florida, called Casa Salsa, a venture he owns with eight Puerto Rican entrepreneurs.

Ricky had incredible success on his tour, attracting audiences of all ages, races, and both sexes. Ricky loves to tour because it really gives him an oppor-

Ricky is a born performer—he thrives on the excitement he gets from being onstage.

❧ Puerto Rican History ❧

It's no mystery that Ricky loves his native Puerto Rico more than just about anything else in the world. It is his first choice for vacationing (Key West, Rio de Janeiro, and the Grand Canyon also rate, however) and he will do just about anything to make sure his homeland is respected and admired throughout the world. It's part of his M.O. "It's all about breaking stereotypes. For me, the fact that people think Puerto Rico is *Scarface*, that we ride donkeys to school—that has to change."

He takes his pride in Puerto Rico very seriously. He even refused to star in a remake of West Side Story with Latina sensation Jennifer Lopez because, as he told *Entertainment Weekly*, "It's kicking my culture. And I'm not gonna feed that."

There have been rumors that once Ricky gets a taste of the American life, he'll want to cross over for good, but he gives those rumors no credence. "I am Puerto Rico," he declared to *Entertainment Weekly*. "The day that happens, I'll quit."

Ricky took part in the official opening of the Puerto-Rican theme Casa Salsa restaurant in South Beach, Florida.

tunity to let loose and go nuts. "I'm very intimate and it is very hard for me to express my feelings in my private life," Ricky says. "I hold everything in; even when I know this could hurt me. I feel I am such an introvert that I need the stage to rid myself of my insecurities, and then I become Superman."

On October 31, 1998, Ricky played for an audience of fourteen thousand screaming fans at Madison Square Garden in New York City. After inciting pandemonium, Ricky closed his concert in the same sweet way he usually does, saying to his swooning fans, "Que Dios los bendiga y la Virgen los acompane" (May God bless you and the Virgin be with you).

Ricky kept touring all over the world, including Asia, at the end of 1998. The marketing coordinator for Epic labels in Japan told *Billboard* magazine that he knew the Japanese were ready for Ricky "because he's good-looking and after receiving all the news from elsewhere that he was doing great, we became very interested in him." And he wasn't kidding. In Singapore, Ricky drew an audience of 4,500 to the Harbour Pavilion. He opened the show by telling his new fans, "I'm going to leave my heart and soul with you on this stage tonight. I hope you do the same, too."

At the end of the year, Ricky toured Europe. In Spain, he recorded a Christmas special for TVE (Television Espanola). He spent New Year's Eve

Ricky brought the house down during his Halloween concert
at Madison Square Garden in New York City.

When asked what he likes most about his career, Ricky replied, "Being onstage. That adrenaline, it's amazing."

Ricky Martin—who else could pull off a silver suit so well?

Did you know...

Ricky is an avid reader. He loves Deepak Chopra, and quotes his philosophies often. He also enjoys the poems of Mario Benedetti, T.S. Eliot, and Garcia Lorca, as well as Gabriel Garcia Marquez, and his two grandmothers'Angel Morales and Iraida Negroni.

performing in Spain with Julio Iglesias, Alejandro Sanz, Shakira, Juam Gabriel, and Joan Manuel Serrat among others. His next trip was to Australia, where he filmed a Pepsi commercial with Janet Jackson.

In January 1999, the National Academy of Recording Arts and Sciences (NARAS) confirmed that Ricky would be one of the performers at the Forty-first Annual Grammy Awards. Other featured performers would include Céline Dion, Whitney Houston and Mariah Carey (singing their new duet), Will Smith, and Madonna. Ricky was also nominated for Best Latin Pop Performance. Michael Greene, President/CEO of the Recording Academy, stated: "We are delighted to have such a talented performer on the Forty-first Annual Grammy Awards. As both an actor and performer, be brings a special energy to the show. We are also committed to represent more Latin music in our endeavors."

It's Show Time!

The Grammys were telecast live from the Shrine Auditorium in Los Angeles, California, on February 24, 1999. Ricky performed his sizzling rendition of "La Copa de la Vida," which would launch him into music history. Ricky set hearts racing and tongues wagging in the audience and throughout the world.

Ricky hams it up at a rehearsal for the 1998 Grammys.

Rebecca de Alba accompanied Ricky to the 1998 Grammy Awards.

That night, Ricky Martin became a household name. It was the most pivotal moment of his career.

Although he exuded enormous confidence, Ricky was really nervous before his performance. "I was anxious at the Grammys," he admitted to *Entertainment Weekly*. "So I said, 'Dude, you've been doing this for fifteen years. Just be yourself.'" And as soon as he began, Ricky knew he was winning his audience over. "They see a Latin guy," he told *Vanity Fair*. "They were expecting the ranchero hat on top of his head, and something modern came out, something very refreshing, very energetic."

When he was done, glistening under the lights, he knew his career and his life would never be the same. "To see Will Smith doing the jiggy with my song!" he beamed to *Time* magazine. "It's overwhelming." But Will Smith wasn't the only one who took notice of Ricky that night. Several doors were about to open.

Did you know...
Ricky said of the Grammys: "I was performing in front of the industry for the first time, and I realized they'd heard and seen it all. I said to myself, 'What are you going to do to catch their attention? Let's give them passion. Let's go out there and be who we are.'"
(*New York Daily News*)

CHAPTER FOUR

Livin' La Vida Loca

After Ricky Martin stole the show at the Grammy Awards, he started to get attention from every direction. "I knew they'd come to me someday," he told *Entertainment Weekly* about the way record executives flocked to him after his performance. "After the Grammys, it was 'Yo, this is mine!'"

The fallout from the Grammy performance was unprecedented. Houston record-store manager Debbie Ratliff told the *Houston Chronicle*, "Ever since he appeared on the Grammys, [Martin's albums have been] blowing out the door. I don't know what those leather pants did. It just, like, turned everybody on. Once it hit that morning, I immediately called the warehouse and ordered a case [each] of the singles and the full-length. We're selling tons of that single."

Another record-store manager, Steve Tiedmann, told the *Chronicle* they "sold out of his album by the weekend [after the Grammys]." Sony president Tommy Mottola told *Entertainment Weekly*, "I haven't seen pandemonium like this since early Springsteen: this is a major cultural movement."

Ricky was discovered by more than just his fans in the Grammy audience. As a special personal coup, he was singled out by Trudie Styler, wife of Sting, a musician Ricky truly admires, to join the lineup at her annual rainforest benefit concert. Ricky was honored to join the ensemble, which included Sting, Tony Bennett, Elton John, and James Taylor, among other huge names in the industry.

Ricky does his own portrayal of Frank Sinatra's "I've Got the World on a String." At the time of this performance—at the Tenth Annual Rainforest Benefit at Carnegie Hall in April 1999—he truly had just that.

Styler decided that for the tenth anniversary show, the performers should all do renditions of Frank Sinatra songs to memorialize the late performer. All were game, including Ricky, who did a tropics-infused rendition of "I've Got the World on String," wearing a gray suit and a porkpie hat.

But Trudie Styler wasn't the only one with her eye on Ricky after the Grammys. The Queen of Pop Music, Madonna herself, could not pry herself from the Latin King's side. When the *Los Angeles Times* questioned Ricky about Madonna's sudden interest in him, he explained, "We had met before. We actually worked together as part of the cast for a TV show in Austria. And we've met a couple of times in Miami. But since [the Grammy Awards] she's been very excited about working with me."

Still euphoric from Ricky's performance, Madonna arranged for the two performers do a duet. The result, "Be Careful" (Cuidada con Mi Corazon), is a lovesick ballad that appears on *Ricky Martin*, Ricky's first solo English-language album. But the making of the single did not go smoothly. *Entertainment Weekly* reported that Mottola was so anxious to get the album out that he rushed Madonna, which prompted her to walk out of the recording. It was Ricky's endearing smile, sweet personality, and charm, no doubt, that brought her back.

Ricky, looking adorable in leather jacket and shades, makes his way to a rehearsal for the Grammys.

Ricky made an appearance at an Oscar party at Morton's restaurant in Los Angeles.

Ricky electrifies an audience of sixty thousand during the three-day Presidente Latin Music Festival in Santa Domingo, Dominican Republic, in June 1998.

Rumors started to fly that the two performers might be romantically involved, in part because of Madonna's love of all things Spanish, but both parties insist that they are just friends.

Finally, on April 20, 1999, it was time for the first single to be released off *Ricky Martin*. "Livin' La Vida Loca" had been getting extensive video and radio play for weeks, teasing a tortured audience that was as yet unable to buy the record. Almost immediately, the song hit No. 1 on the *Billboard* Hot Latin Tracks and Pop Chart. It debuted at No. 54 on the *Billboard* Hot 100 chart. "With all humbleness," Ricky told *Entertainment Weekly*, "I think we'll sell a million copies."

On April 22, Ricky performed at the *Billboard* Latin Music Awards ceremony, hosted by Daisy Fuentes and Paul Rodriguez and held in Miami, Florida. He took home another award, a statue for Pop Album of the Year, Male, for *Vuelve*.

Ricky Martin was finally released May 11, 1999, and it obviously wasn't just an impulsive maneuver sparked by the attention Ricky received after the

The Latin Revolution

Some have said that Ricky Martin is really paving the way for Latin performers. Well, that may be true, at least for the new wave. Desmond Child, co-writer of "Livin' La Vida Loca," told *Entertainment Weekly* that "Latin stars have been trying to cross over for a long time. A lot of it just sits there. Ricky's a prince who's been groomed to be a king."

The industry seems to be primed and ready now and looking for a little passion and spice in its melodies. In fact, Latin music sales rose rose 16 percent in 1998, to $571 million, according to *Entertainment Weekly*.

Gloria Estefan broke new ground for Latin artists when she burst onto the scene with the Miami Sound Machine in the mid-1980s. "When their first hit came out, everybody was shakin' their bodies, doin' the conga." After a few years, Gloria dropped the Machine and achieved tremendous success as a solo artist.

Dashing and dapper, Ricky Martin mugs for a photographer during the Vanity Fair *Oscar party.*

Ricky loves his fans as much as they love him. Here, he signs autographs for admirers at a signing at Tower Records in New York City on May 11, 1999.

The next Latina superstar to emerge was Selena. If a crazed fan had not cut her life short just as she was about to enter the English market she probably would have had an incredible impact on the U.S. music scene. The fact that a film about her tragic life story achieved a wide release after her death is ample evidence that she would have been a huge hit.

Now that Ricky has opened the door for the next wave, you can expect to hear more and more Latin rhythms coming over the radio. Talents like Marc Anthony, who described his summer 1998 release as "not salsa, not dance, just pop" to *Time* magazine, are out there, just not in the mainstream. In fact, when Anthony went to look for his album in a record store at Times Square, he was told to look in the international section. "I recorded it on 47th Street! How much more local can you get than that?" he asked.

In March, *Seventeen* magazine did a profile called "The Fab Five," which profiled the five sexiest stars of Latin music, from

At the World Music Awards in Monaco, May 1995. Ricky bows before paparazzi in the pressroom.

Ricky Martin, who opened the piece, to Charles Zaa, Alejandro Fernandez, Marc Anthony, and Carlos Ponce. And that's not all. Newspapers and magazines everywhere have spotted the trend, giving these Latin soon-to-be-stars a push toward stardom.

By no measure have the women been left out of this wave. Hollywood actress Jennifer Lopez has just made the crossover into music, while the singer Shakira, still unknown in the United States and Canada but preparing to make her debut this summer, recently told *Time* that her album will "demonstrate to the rest of the world that Latin people also can make good pop and good rock."

Sony head Tommy Mottola has a lot of confidence in the Latin Revolution. "I have no crystal ball," he told *Time*, "but my gut tells me that Latin music can be the next big reservoir of talent for mainstream superstars."

In 1999 Ricky was honored at the World Music Awards in Monaco.

Grammys. "We've been making this record for two and a half years," Joanna Ifrah, A&R director at Columbia, told *Rolling Stone*. "There's a million ways we could have gone, but we sat down and said, 'What are we going to do that's different? No Backstreet Boys or 'N Sync kind of sound.' He was already huge everywhere else, but no one had heard of him here. It was very important to keep the Latin feel."

The album's release, as expected, triggered a frenzy among Ricky fans everywhere. Ricky went to New York and performed on *Saturday Night Live* on May 8—sharing billing with host Monica Lewinsky. Ricky spent the week of May 10 running around the city, hitting the morning talk show circuit. He chatted in perfect English with Katie Couric on the *Today* show and with one of his earliest celebrity fans, Rosie O'Donnell.

And that is just the beginning of Ricky fever.

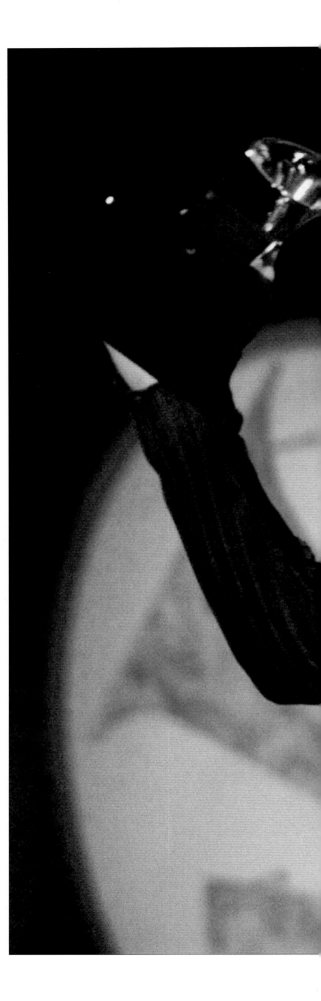

Gorgeous Ricky, not holding back any smiles, accepts his Grammy for Vuelve.

Fans lined the streets and waited in line for hours just to catch a glimpse of Ricky when he appeared at Tower Records in New York City in May of 1999.

Conclusion

So what are Ricky's plans for the future? "Right now my album is my priority. But if something with Demi Moore shows up, maybe I am going to have to think about it," he admits. He also told *Vanity Fair,* "You know, maybe tomorrow the best freaking script will show up with the best director and the best cast and I'm gonna think about it." But for now, it's all about the music.

Does the avalanche of success look like it will bury Martin? Not hardly. He hasn't even begun to enjoy his new worldwide fame. And quitting is a long way off. He told the *Los Angeles Times,* "Whenever I feel like throwing in the towel, I say to myself: 'If you quit, you're never going to be able to go to another show, because if you do, you're gonna feel so envious you won't know what to do. You're gonna think: 'I could have been there, I could have been that person who's there now.' That's what keeps me from quitting."

Ricky tries hard to keep his feet planted firmly on the ground. "Fame can be fatal," he told the *New York Daily News.* "The day [that] life is not fun anymore, I quit. I swear. Before, I was working to forget about problems in life. Today I'm working because I'm having a good time." Let's hope he keeps having a good time for a long, long time to come!

Ricky wants you to go out there and start "Livin' La Vida Loca."

Discography

Albums

Ricky Martin, 1991, Sony Discos
Me Amarás, 1993, Discos CBS
    International
A Medio Vivir, 1995, Sony
Vuelve, 1998, Sony International
Ricky Martin, 1999, Columbia

Singles

"Maria," 1996, Columbia
"1 2 3 Maria," 1997, Sony
"Cup of Life," 1998, Sony
"La Bomba, Part 2," 1999
"Livin' La Vida Loca" [Australia],
    1999
"Livin' La Vida Loca" [U.S.], 1999

Songs

Ricky Martin (1991)

"Fuego Contra Fuego"
"Dime Que Me Quieres"
"Vuelo"
"Conmigo Nadie Puede"
"Te Voy a Conquistar"
"Juego de Ajedrez"
"Corazon Entre Nubes"
"Ser Feliz"
"El Amor de Mi Vida"
"Susana"
"Popotitos"

A Medio Vivir (1995)

"Fuego de Noche, Nieve de Dia"
"A Medio Vivir"
"Maria"
"Te Extrano, Te Olvido, Te Amo"
"Donde Estaras"
"Volveras"
"Revolucion"
"Somos la Semilla"
"Como Decirte Adios"
"Bombom de Azucar"
"Corazon"
"Nada Es Imposible"

Me Amarás, 1993

"No Me Pidas Mas"
"Es Mejor Decirse Adios"
"Entre el Amor Y los Halagos"
"Lo Que Nos Pase, Pasara"
"Ella Es"
"Me Amarás"
"Ayudame"
"Eres Como el Aire"
"Que Dia Es Hoy"
"Hooray! Hooray! (It's a Holi-
Holiday)"

Vuelve, 1998

"Por Arriba, Por Abajo"
"Vuelve"
"Lola, Lola"
"Casi Un Bolero"

"Corazonado"
"La Bomba"
"Hagamos el Amor"
"La Copa de la Vida"
"Perdido Sin Ti"
"Asi Es la Vida"
"Marcia Baila"
"No Importa la Distancia"
"Gracias Por Pensar en Mi"
"Casi Un Bolero"

Ricky Martin, 1999

"Livin' La Vida Loca"
"Spanish Eyes"
"She's All I Ever Had"
"Shake Your Bon-Bon"
"Be Careful (Cuidado Con
    Mi Corazon)"
"I Am Made of You"
"Love You for a Day"
"Private Emotion (Duet with Meja)"
"The Cup of Life"
"You Stay with Me"
"I Count the Minutes"
"Bella (She's All I Ever Had)"
"Maria"

Photo Credits

Bibliography

Periodicals

Castro, Peter. "From Menudo to Manhood." *People Weekly*. (May 15, 1995): 109.

Devine, Peter. "Boogie Night." *Vanity Fair*. (June 1999): 152.

Dominguez, Robert. "Latin Heartthrob Is the New Craze." *The Long Island Daily News*. (May 11, 1999).

Essex, Andrew. "Not So Little Ricky." *Entertainment Weekly*. (April 23, 1999): 33-35.

"The Fab Five." *Seventeen*. (March 1999): 138-144

Farley, Christoper John. "Get Ready for Ricky." *Time*. (May 10, 1999): 84.

"The 50 Most Beautiful People in the World." *People Weekly*. (May 10, 1999): 92.

Goodman, Fred. "La explosion pop Latino." *Rolling Stone*. (May 13, 1999): 21-22.

Guerra, Joey. "Heartthrob's Music Soars." *Houston Chronicle*. (March 8, 1999): 1

Harrington, Richard. "Boys to Men." *The Washington Post*. (May 9, 1999): G08.

Lannert, John. "Sony's Ricky Martin Is Making Waves." *Billboard*. (February 14, 1999): 9.

Lechner, Ernesto. "Rising From the Ashes of Menudo and Tempered by a New Maturity, Ricky Martin Is Latin Pop's Numero Uno." *Los Angeles Times*. (October 12, 1998): 6

Lorenz, Christian. "Sony's Ricky Martin, Youssou N'Dour Chosen to Provide World Cup Music." *Billboard*. (December 20, 1997): 76.

Ross, Karl. "Song Tanned in Political Cause." *Billboard*. (September 5, 1999): 10.

Tayler, Letta. "Crooning, Clowning at Salute to Sinatra." *Los Angeles Times*. (April 19, 1999): F-3

Thigpen, David E. "Spicing the Mix." *Time*. (March 15, 1999).

Worldwide Web

Cramer, Christina. "Ricky Martin." *Rolling Stone* online.

Ghorbani, Liza. "Raves: Ricky Martin." *Rolling Stone* online.

Guillen, Gypsy. "Ricky Martin in Concert Madison Square Garden." *Latin Music* online.

Lim, Rebecca. "Ricky Martin *Vuelve* Asian Tour." *Latin Music* online.

Little Judy. "Ricky Martin in Concert Radio City Music Hall, March 30, 1996." *LatinMusic* online.

Little Judy. "Ricky Martin In-Store Appearance Virgin Megastore, NYC." *Latin Music* online.

Little Judy. "Ricky Martin in *Les Misérables*." *Latin Music* online.

Little Judy. "Ricky Martin: Soul of a Young Artist." *Latin Music* online.

"Menudo." T.E.I. Corporate Entertainment Professionals.

"Ricky Martin Launches First Puerto Rican Theme Restaurant." Rickymartin.vuelve.com.

"Ricky Martin Makes a Show-Stopping Debut at the 41st Annual Grammy Awards." Rickymartin.vuelve.com.

"Ricky Martin in Taipei." *Latin Music* online.

"Ricky Martin on Top of the World with: Sting, Elton John, and Billy Joel." Rickymartin.vuelve.com.

"Ricky Martin Will Perform "La Copa de la Vida" on the 41st Annual Grammy Awards on February 24 on CBS." Rickymartin.vuelve.com.

"…and the World Discovered Ricky Martin." Rickymartin.vuelve.com.

Write to Ricky:

Ricky Martin International Fan Club
P.O. Box 13345, Santurce Station, San Juan, Puerto Rico, E-mail: Rickym@coqui.net

Visit Ricky:

www.rickymartin.coqui.net, *www.rickymartin.com*, *www.c2records.com*, *www.columbiarecords.com*

Index